JAMESTOWN EDUCATION

inClass Reader

TREK 1

Jamestown READING NAVIGATOR

McGraw Hill **Glencoe**

New York, New York   Columbus, Ohio   Chicago, Illinois   Peoria, Illinois   Woodland Hills, California

JAMESTOWN 🚢 EDUCATION

Send all inquiries to:
Glencoe/McGraw-Hill
8787 Orion Place
Columbus, OH 43240-4027

ISBN-13: 978-0-07-861036-3
ISBN-10: 0-07-861036-2

Printed in the United States of America.

2 3 4 5 6 7 8 9 10 110 11 10 09 08 07 06

Photo Credits

Contents

Unit 1   Why Should I Read? 5

▶ May Day 6

▶ Winter X Games 10

▶ Ray's Rock 14

▶ Nitaya's Quest 18

Unit 2   Who Can I Count On? 22

▶ Paul, the Hero 23

▶ What Is a Real Friend? 28

▶ Elana, the Leader 33

▶ Lost in the Snow 39

Unit 3   What Do I Want Most?................45

▶ Water Power 46

▶ She Knows What She Wants 53

▶ Time to Heal 60

▶ The Helping Machine 68

Why Should I Read?

MAY DAY

Can you sing? Are you good? Can you go fast? Can you go slow? Are you on time? If so, we need you.

We are a band. Our name is May Day. We are the best. We play funk. We play pop. We play rock. We know lots of songs. We play well. We drill and drill. We stop when it is right.

We meet each day. We meet in 222. We play from 6 to 8. Be there.

Hink Pink

A Hink Pink is a riddle. The answer is 2 words that rhyme.
Look at the example. Then do your own Hink Pink.
Choose words from the word box.

hip	zip	ship	tip	lip	trip

Example:

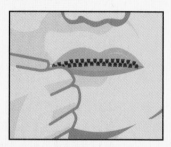

Clue: What do you do when you shut your mouth?

Answer: zip lip

1. **Clue:** What do you call a ride on a boat?

   Answer: a _____ _____

2. **Clue:** What is a clue to where to hear cool music?

   Answer: a _____ _____

What Did You Read?

1. What is the name of the band?

   _____

   _____

   _____

   _____

2. What days do they play?

   _____

   _____

   _____

   _____

Winter X Games

Can a man fly? He can in the X Games! The X **athletes** go to Colorado. They ride the hills. They do tricks on the snow. They are the best.

Brian Deegan sails on his bike. Up he goes. One hand is on. One hand is off.

Brian Deegan

---

athletes people who are the best in sports

Simon Dumont drops flat on the trail. He jumps. He bends. Up is down. Down is up.

Shaun White has a board. He is on top. He falls fast. But he pops up 20 feet!

Blair Morgan feels free on his sled. It runs like a race car. It is that fast.

Yes, a man can fly today. The deal is to flip and drop. But not to spill.

Word Drop

This story has missing words.
On line 1, drop in a word from box 1.
On line 2, drop in a word from box 2, and so on.

Line	Words to Choose From		
1	see	flee	smell
2	bee	cone	tree
3	trot	flip	smile
4	hot	flat	right

I fell in the snow! I did not _____

                                            1

that _____ . Next time, I'll show you

                        2

my best _____ . I will do

                            3

it _____ . "

                  4

What Did You Read?

1. What do the athletes do tricks on?

   _____

   _____

   _____

   _____

2. What does *spill* mean in the story?

   _____

   _____

   _____

   _____

Ray's Rock

Josefina Bell teaches in Salinas. It is a farming town. She knows a bright boy. His name is Ray. He is in the tenth grade. He is not here today.

"I know where he is," says Bell. "He is picking grapes. He goes away each fall. Then he comes back. I do not like it. That is just the way it is."

A vineyard is a piece of land where grapes are grown.

There are lots of boys like Ray. They go from farm to farm. They grow crops. Some go back to Mexico. They may go to school. They may not.

"It is a problem," says Bell. "Many drop out. But Ray is bright. He is good in math. I will help him."

Ray will catch up. He will take classes at lunch. He will take classes in summer. He will do what it takes. Josefina Bell knows this. She is Ray's rock.

Rhyme Time

Read the rhyme. Add the missing words.
Hint: **they both end in** *-ail,* **like** *Gail.*

I know a bright girl named Gail.

She lost a race with a _____ .
₁

She knew she was slow,

and her feet did not go.

But she won when she fell on its _____ !
₂

Think of another ending for the rhyme.

Write it below:

_____

_____

_____

What Did You Read?

1. Why is Ray not in class?

   _____

   _____

   _____

   _____

2. What is Ray's best class?

   _____

   _____

   _____

   _____

3. What does *rock* mean in this story?

   _____

   _____

   _____

   _____

Nitaya's Quest

This is Nitaya. She is from Thailand. She is new to our school. She is our guest. Smile when you see her!

Nitaya will see the U.S. She is on a **quest.** She will be the best in English. This is what she says.

"At first I felt alone. I always called my mom. I was not all right. But time went on. I knew this was a test. I will not fail. I will do my best."

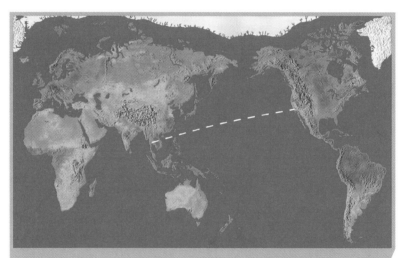

Nitaya came more than 8,000 miles to the U.S.

quest something you seek

"You do real well," I tell her. "Who do you stay with? Are they all right?"

"I stay with Eva Lopez. She is my new mom for a while," smiles Nitaya. "She is fun. She shows me a lot. I can make a **Mexican** meal. I know a few Spanish words."

That is a deal. Nitaya will see the U.S. She will be the best in English. And she will get Spanish for free!

Mexican from Mexico

Word Find

Find these words. Circle them.
They can be down, slanted, or side to side.

Sounds like *rain*	Sounds like *meet*	Sounds like *pile*	Sounds like *no*	Sounds like *soon*
gate	bead	dime	bone	spoon
lane	deal	right	know	new
mail	feet	ride	code	
stain	neat	tile	scope	
way				

a	r	g	a	t	e	s	b	p	s
b	c	r	i	d	e	p	o	n	c
e	o	i	n	i	t	o	n	r	o
a	d	a	l	m	l	o	e	i	p
d	e	a	l	e	r	n	w	g	e
k	n	o	w	a	y	t	m	h	n
f	e	e	t	l	n	e	a	t	t
r	s	t	a	i	n	e	i	y	u
w	a	o	b	c	l	q	l	m	g
r	s	b	l	v	p	e	c	d	s

What Did You Read?

1. What is Nitaya's quest?

   _____

   _____

   _____

   _____

2. How does she feel at first?

   _____

   _____

   _____

   _____

3. What does Nitaya get in the end?

   _____

   _____

   _____

   _____

Unit 2

Who Can I Count On?

Paul, the Hero

Did you see the movie *Hotel Rwanda?* It tells how Paul Rusesabagina saved more than 1,200 people. Who was this **hero?** How did he save people?

Paul Rusesabagina was born on June 15, 1954, in Rwanda. Rwanda is a country in Africa. Paul lived on a farm. He did not seem like a hero. He just did his best.

When he grew up, Paul wanted to run a **hotel.** So he went to school to learn how. He did well. But he did not seem like a hero then.

When Paul was 30, it was time to run a hotel on his own. He went to work for the Mille Collines Hotel. It was a very nice hotel in Kigali, Rwanda. He did his best. But he still did not seem like a hero.

---

hero a brave person
hotel a building where people pay to eat meals and sleep

Don Cheadle played the part of Paul Rusesabagina in the 2004 movie *Hotel Rwanda.*

In 1994 war came to Rwanda. Soon the people had to flee to Paul's hotel. Men with guns were chasing them. They needed a safe place to stay.

"May we stay?" they said. "We are not safe."

"Yes, you may," Paul said with a smile. "It is not too late."

For 100 days Paul let the people stay in the hotel. Many people in Rwanda died in the war. But the people in the hotel were safe. Now Paul seems like a hero.

When people say Paul is a hero, he says, "I just did what was right. No one should hate."

But Paul is a hero to 1,200 people. He saved their lives!

Paul and his wife, Tatiana, answer questions at the White House in 2005.

Hink Pink

A Hink Pink is a riddle. The answer is 2 words that rhyme.
Look at the example. Then do your own Hink Pink.
Choose words from the word box.

meat	trunk	plate	junk	late	treat

Example:

Clue: What is beef or pork to eat as a snack?

Answer: a meat treat

1. **Clue:** What is a big box filled with things nobody wants?

   Answer: a _____ _____

2. **Clue:** What is a dish that is not on time?

   Answer: a _____ _____

What Did You Read?

1. What is Rwanda?

   _____

   _____

   _____

   _____

2. Why did 1,200 people need help?

   _____

   _____

   _____

   _____

3. Why is Paul a hero?

   _____

   _____

   _____

   _____

What Is a Real Friend?

Real friends are hard to come by. You know them by what they do. What does a real friend do? It is not the same for all people. Take Sam. For him, a real friend is one he can trust.

"I have a friend named Tim," says Sam. "One time, I told him a secret. It was about Jane. I told him not to tell."

But Tim did tell. He told Jan and Jan told Pam. Soon, it was all over the school.

"I was not mad at Tim," says Sam. "I did not mope. It was time to let go. I spent more time with other people. Friends come and go. It is no big deal."

Sam knows who is *not* a friend. Julia, on the other hand, knows who *is* a friend. "A real friend," she says, "stays with you when others flee." She remembers the day she fell ill.

"I have a friend. Her name is Gabe. We gab on the phone all night. One day, I was at her house. Her mom had made this stew. I ate two big bowls of it. Soon, I felt bad. I felt real bad," says Julia.

"In no time, I was on my knees. I had a tight grip on the seat. Kat and Jen ran away in disgust. I have a gripe with them. Gabe stayed. She held my hair up. She stayed until it was over."

Would Tim have stayed if it had been Sam?

"Are you kidding? Not only that," notes Sam, "but he would have made me mop."

Word Drop

This story has missing words.
On line 1, drop in a word from box 1.
On line 2, drop in a word from box 2, and so on.

Line	Words to Choose From		
1	hope	hop	know
2	bit	bite	deal
3	pine	pin	note
4	smell	smile	mope

I miss you, dear friend! I _____ you are well.
                                    1

Tell me a _____ of good news. Drop me
                    2

a _____. That would truly make
            3

me _____.
            4

What Did You Read?

1. How does Sam feel about friends?

_____

_____

_____

_____

2. Gabe is a real friend. Why?

_____

_____

_____

_____

3. Why does Julia have a gripe with Kat and Jen?

_____

_____

_____

_____

Elana, the Leader

The town of Pikesville, Maryland, is like a lot of others. It has schools and libraries. It has hospitals. There are stores, too. There are places to swim. There are parks. There are other places to play outside.

Pikesville is like a lot of **communities** in another way, too. There are people who need help. A lot of communities need leaders. Pikesville needs leaders, too. Who do you think most leaders are? Did you say leaders are **adults?** Then you are partly right. But one leader in Pikesville comes from a high school. Her name is Elana Brownstein.

---

communities all the people who live in certain places
adults grown-up people

Elana helped her community for a long time. She started long before she was 16 years old. She got a lot of prizes. But Elana wanted to do more than give her own time. She liked to get other teens to help with her ideas too.

Elana saw many bad ads for clothes. The ads made some girls feel bad. The ads say only thin is good. Elana found out about GO GIRLS. This is a good program that teaches girls not to look at bad ads. Elana and her friends talked to people who run the stores. They said they would show nice clothes for girls. The clothes would look good on all body shapes and sizes.

In 2002, Elana helped start a new program. It was called For the Love of Children. This program found things for children who had no parents. Elana looked for the main things that the children needed. Having these things gave the children hope for a better life.

Elana Brownstein visits a hospital in Haifa, Israel.

A group of children learn about the Jewish way of life.

Elana even went to Hungary! She worked at a summer camp there. A lot of **Jewish** children went to the camp. But the children did not know what it means to be a Jew. There are many things to learn. It is a way of life. Elana told the children what she knew about being a Jew in the United States.

Elana hopes to be a community leader all her life. Elana helps make our country great!

Jewish having to do with a group who follow very old ideas that began in the Middle East

Rhyme Time

Read the rhyme. Add the missing words.
Hint: **they end in** *-ime* **like** *crime* **or** *-ate* **like** *plate.*

My clock has a loud chime.

It rings at the right _____ .
 1

It helps to not be late.

When I know I have a _____ !
 2

Think of another ending for the rhyme.

Write it below:

_____

_____

_____

What Did You Read?

1. How is Pikesville like a lot of communities?

   _____

   _____

   _____

2. How does GO GIRLS help the community?

   _____

   _____

   _____

3. When did Elana help start For the Love of Children?

   _____

   _____

   _____

4. What is a community leader?

   _____

   _____

   _____

Lost in the Snow

It was February 6, 2004. Eric LeMarque was having fun at Mammoth Mountain. A pro on the snowboard, he was going for a last run. Then he would hop into a hot tub. But it was not a short run. It took him seven days to get back.

Mammoth Mountain in California is a popular ski area.

Day 1

At the end of the slope, Eric knew he was lost. He was alone in a **vast** forest. He had not packed a meal. He had not left a note. He had no phone or light. He had an MP3 player and some gum.

Eric walked for miles. He did not have his best socks, and his feet got wet. When night fell, he dug a hole in the snow with his board. He lined it with bark and went to sleep.

Day 2

The next day, he hiked some more. He drank from a river. There, he saw a tin can. He chopped it to bits. "If I pin this tin on, the sun will **reflect** off it," he said to himself. "I hope someone sees me soon."

Eric had to eat. He knew that if he ate snow, his body heat would drop. So with his board he cut tree bark. He ate that and pine nuts. Then he went to sleep.

---

vast very large
reflect to send back light

Day 3

By this time, Eric's feet were black and bleeding. He peeled his socks off, and some skin came off. Still, he had to hike up. He used his board as a cane. A plane flew by. Eric flipped on his MP3 player. The plan was for the plane to see the blue light. But it was no use.

Day 4

When Eric woke, he found he was stuck in snow. He yelled and waved his arms until he was free. Now he was mad. He made his way up with all his rage. He would look for people. Then he would slide down to them. He did not make it.

Days 5 and 6

Eric could not get up. His body was slowly shutting down. He was a fine athlete, but this was too much.

Eric LeMarque leaves the hospital.

Day 7

Today was Friday the 13th, Eric's lucky day. Some men in a **chopper** had seen him! They got him up with a rope.

Eric was very weak. He had lost 35 pounds. In the hospital, they cut off his **frozen** feet. Eric is learning to walk on new feet. He can not wait to go back up on Mammoth Mountain.

---

chopper a helicopter, or flying machine with large blades on top that turn very fast to make it fly
frozen very cold

Word Find

Find these words. Circle them.
They can be down, slanted, or side to side.

Sounds like *pain*	Sounds like *eat*	Sounds like *pile*	Sounds like *no*	Sounds like *too*
cane	weak	fine	note	flew
ate	free	mile	slope	soon
rage	peel	night	snow	
day	me	light	alone	
		time	rope	

p	e	e	l	b	d	p	f	s	r
c	m	e	c	d	n	a	n	l	w
a	i	a	t	e	i	o	y	o	e
n	l	i	e	y	g	f	w	p	f
e	e	l	i	g	h	t	r	e	i
r	a	g	e	t	t	i	s	e	n
a	l	o	n	e	n	n	e	a	e
w	e	a	k	n	o	j	e	l	t
s	o	o	n	w	t	f	l	e	w
a	b	r	o	p	e	t	i	m	e

What Did You Read?

1. What did Eric have with him on Day 1?

   _____

   _____

   _____

2. What did he do with the tin can?

   _____

   _____

   _____

3. What did Eric eat?

   _____

   _____

   _____

4. What did Eric want to do when he healed?

   _____

   _____

   _____

What Do I Want Most?

Water Power

The girls are ready for the swim meet. They get on their mark, the horn sounds, and they dive in. Adanech Spratlin starts out on par with the others. She swims with power and **grace.** Slowly, she inches ahead. The people who are watching jump up and shout with joy. Adanech wins!

The way she swam, no one would even know Adanech has only one arm and one leg.

Born in Ethiopia, Adanech grew up in **poverty** with her grandmother. One day, Adanech was walking home along some train tracks. She slipped in the mud and fell on the tracks, just as a train was coming. Her right arm was cut off by the wheels. Her right leg was **maimed** too, and later it had to be taken off.

---

grace a smooth way of moving
poverty the state of being very poor
maimed injured very badly

Adanech's grandmother could not take care of her. She was sick and had no way to pay for Adanech's doctors. At last, her grandmother had to plead for help. A children's help worker, Yonas Kebede, answered the call. Kebede says he saw something special in the girl.

"When I met her for the first time, I could see it in her eyes," said Kebede. "She is just brave."

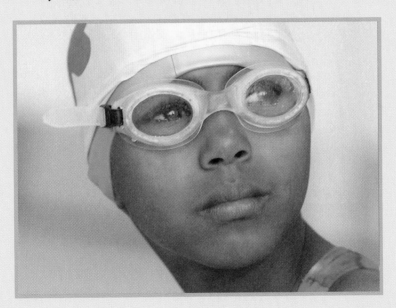

Kebede put Adanech on a flight to Atlanta, Georgia. He had doctors fit Adanech for an **artificial** leg at a hospital. The doctors worked for free. Adanech stayed with Jeff and Paige Spratlin and their children, Ellis, Aaron, and Avery. At first, Adanech was afraid. "I did not know what would happen to me," she said. The Spratlins soon fell in love with this brave little girl. Her grandmother agreed to let the Spratlins **adopt** Adanech.

Adanech runs in Atlanta's Peachtree Jr. 2-mile race.

---

artificial not real but made to be like something that is real
adopt to take someone else's child into your home and become his or her parent

Adanech learned to swim in the family pool.

Adanech's brothers often swam in the backyard pool. Adanech grew tired of sitting, so she jumped into the water too. She learned to swim, one might say, about as well as a trout. She felt free in the water and became a star swimmer at school.

"She is one student I will remember the rest of my life," said one teacher.

She is not even a teen yet, but Adanech has gained a bit of fame. When Oprah Winfrey heard about Adanech's story, she invited Adanech to be on the show! Adanech was quite cool on the stage, and not at all meek or shy. She smiled warmly, and Oprah **stroked** Adanech's dark, curly braids. The talk show host was very happy with her little guest.

---

stroked made a slow and easy movement with the hand

Adanech says she is no more special than anyone else, and that we can all do great things. To kids who go through hard times, she says this: "You should give it a try. Work hard, . . . and then if you just do not get it, someday you will."

Hink Pink

A Hink Pink is a riddle. The answer is 2 words that rhyme. Look at the example. Then do your own Hink Pink. Choose words from the word box.

saw	cry	shark	sky	paw	dark

Example:

Clue: What is a big fish that is hard to see?

Answer: a dark shark

1. **Clue:** What would a dog use to build a house?

   Answer: a _____ _____

2. **Clue:** What is another name for a rain storm?

   Answer: a _____ _____

What Did You Read?

1. Where was Adanech born?

   _____

   _____

2. Why did she go to Georgia?

   _____

   _____

3. Who is Yonas Kebede?

   _____

   _____

4. How did Adanech feel when she first came
   to the United States?

   _____

   _____

5. What is Adanech's claim to fame?

   _____

   _____

She Knows What She Wants

Do you have something you dream about? What is it? What would it take to make your dream come true? This is a story about a girl who knew what she wanted and went after it.

Kenya Jordana James was a big dreamer. But that was not enough for her. She had to find a way to make her dreams fly. In 2002, when Kenya was twelve years old, she started her own **magazine.** She called it *Blackgirl*. It is a magazine for teenage girls.

---

magazine a large, thin book with a paper cover

Kenya Jordana James

Why did Kenya start the magazine? When she was in grade school, Kenya did not like the magazines that were aimed at girls. Most of them did not write the kind of stories she wanted to read. She did not want to read just about music and movie stars. She wanted to read about other things too, like **history** and **culture.**

It took quite a lot of toil to begin the first stage. Kenya had $1,200 she had raised from selling cakes she had made. That was a major start, but she knew she also needed a real plan, so she made one.

---

history things that happened in the past
culture way of life that is shared by people

She wrote down what she needed to know and what she wanted the magazine to be. She thought about how much money she needed to start and how she was going to get it.

Kenya's mom helped. She told Kenya she believed she could do it, so Kenya went to work on her plan. She learned what she needed to know. She learned about other magazines. Kenya did not want her magazine to be a clone of all the others. She worked hard in English class, and she went to a camp for writers. She learned how to sell ads for the magazine. She found first-rate people to work with her and get the word out. All of this helped to get the magazine up and running.

Kenya's magazine is a hip mix. It has stories about people who have fame and power. It also has stories about the bright lights of sports and music. History and culture have a place in Kenya's magazine too. And to top it all off, *Blackgirl* pops with page after page of pictures.

Blackgirl has won many prizes. It has caused a spark with girls all over the country. Kenya lives in Atlanta, but she travels from town to town and speaks to groups. She even has been on television!

Kenya talks to teens all the time and explains to them the joy of dreaming big. She talks to adults too, and she tells them that teens can do anything they put their minds to. Kenya knows how much it means for girls to discover what they can do. Kenya says that if you find something you are good at, you should keep doing it. That is, until you find another thing you want to do as much! Kenya Jordana James should know — no one can stop you but yourself.

Word Drop

This story has missing words.
On line 1, drop in a word from box 1.
On line 2, drop in a word from box 2, and so on.

Line	Words to Choose From		
1	cry	try	shy
2	sorry	happy	funny
3	log	dog	bog
4	oil	spoil	boil

Some people say that I am _____ . I don't
1

know why because I am really _____ . One time
2

I fell off of a _____ just for a smile. Nothing
3

can _____ my fun.
4

What Did You Read?

1. How old was Kenya when she started
   her magazine?

   _____

   _____

2. What is the name of her magazine?

   _____

   _____

3. Why did Kenya start her magazine?

   _____

   _____

4. How did Kenya learn how to run a magazine?

   _____

   _____

5. What does Kenya tell adults about teens?

   _____

   _____

Time to Heal

One evening, Nomar was driving his friend
Rasheed home from a party. A light rain was
falling, and the road was slippery. As Nomar and
Rasheed came around a turn, their small car **veered**
right into the path of a truck. The truck driver was
not harmed. Rasheed was killed, though, and we
had little hope that Nomar would **survive.**

When Nomar woke up, he could not move.
His lean, 17-year-old body was broken — and
his **spirit** was broken too. What would he tell
Rasheed's family? Would they blame him? He
wanted to sleep and not wake up.

---

veered changed direction
survive to stay alive
spirit zest for life

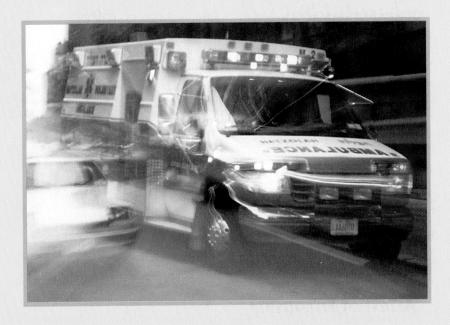

   As his doctor, it was my job to help Nomar, to clean him up and stay close by. I did whatever I could to help **relieve** his pain. I knew that for Nomar to heal, he had to be well in body and in spirit. I could help heal his broken body. But to mend his broken spirit, he needed the love of friends and family. They were just as important to his care as I was.

---

relieve to make less

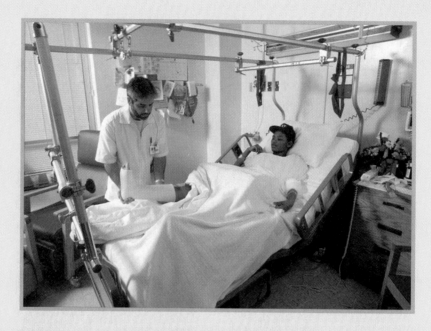

A Test of Friendship

For the first few days, many people Nomar knew found the time to wander in with gifts and **chat** and tell funny stories. But after a while they stopped coming. They could not deal with Nomar's bad mood — he was in a major funk. They did not feel they could help him, either. Nomar did not look the same, and he could not cope with the fact that he might never be the same. Nomar knew why people wanted to shy away from him.

---

chat to talk in a friendly way

Who could blame them? Nomar's skin was gray. His eyes were sunk deep, his jaw was tight, and his cheek bones stuck out. Steel rods held his bones in place. He was weak and in pain. Who but his family would want to be near him?

Nomar had one faithful friend. Her name was Carmen, a sweet, soft-spoken girl. She and Nomar knew each other best when they were children. They had gone different ways in high school, but here she was now. And she came every day. If Nomar would cry, Carmen would cry too. If Nomar wanted to shout, Carmen nodded. Carmen let Nomar claim whatever feelings he needed to get out. Sometimes he was mean and he would pout, and I thought, "This boy is going to destroy a very good thing." But Carmen did not **falter.**

---

falter to become unable to continue

Time to Heal

Little by little, Nomar began to feel better, and his mood **improved.** He let his needs be known, but always with a smile. "Doctor Choi," he would say, "What time is it?" After a few days he asked for a straw, and a week later he asked for some pie. Finally he said, "I want to go home."

---

improved became better

Nomar still had to come to the hospital for **therapy.** I went about my work. Then one day I was looking out the window, and I saw Carmen pushing Nomar in the wheelchair. Nomar still had both of his legs in casts, but each one now had a colorful racing stripe. Suddenly Carmen hopped onto the back of his chair, and they coasted down the driveway. They rode the long, gentle slope together all the way to the end.

therapy the treatment of an illness or injury over a long period of time

Rhyme Time

Read the rhyme. Add the missing words.
Hint: they both end in *-ark,* like *spark.*

I have a big dog named Shark.

He likes to spend time at the _____ .

He barks at the trees

and runs in the breeze.

We stay there until it gets _____ .

Think of another ending for the rhyme.

Write it below:

_____

_____

_____

What Did You Read?

1. What happened to Nomar?

   _____

   _____

2. Why did people stop coming to visit Nomar?

   _____

   _____

3. How did Doctor Choi help Nomar?

   _____

   _____

4. How did Carmen help Nomar?

   _____

   _____

5. What happened soon after Nomar went home?

   _____

   _____

The Helping Machine

Hanna and Heather Craig are teens who share a special trait: They like to find out how things work. When they were growing up in Alaska, the **identical twins** liked to take things apart. They also liked to build things — small machines that they could operate with hand-held controls. As they got better at it, they talked about how smart it was to let **robots** do hard jobs instead of people doing them. When they were just 15 years old, the sisters had a bright idea. Why not build a robot that could help people who fall through the ice?

---

identical twins twins that come from the same egg and are the same sex

robots machines that can move and do some of the work of a person, and are often run by a computer

   Hanna and Heather know about the dangers of ice. Alaska is in a cold zone. The winters there are colder than in most places. A person who falls through the ice into the water can die in just moments. It is important for helpers to get the **victims** out of the cold water fast! But going out on the ice is a **danger** for helpers, too. If the helpers fall through, it just adds to the problem.

---

victims people who have had something bad happen to them
danger the chance that someone or something will be harmed or killed

Heather (left) and Hanna show off their "helping machine."

The robot would have to be very light, so it would not break through the ice. It would have to move on its own, without anyone riding on it. It would have to be safe on the ice and not slide around. It would have to be able to "see" where the victims are. It would have to carry a rope to the victims and pull them out of the water.

Hanna and Heather knew that having a good idea was the easy part. The hard part was to build something that would not fail.

The twins looked around for things they could use. They were already good at making **gadgets** out of odds and ends. They made the robot parts out of old bike and car parts. Most of the parts had to be changed a little to make them work. The sisters named the robot they built the Ice Crawler.

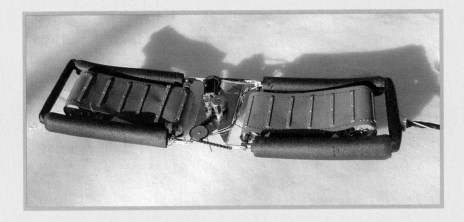

gadgets small, useful machines or tools

The girls made the robot very light so it would not fall through thin ice. The robot runs on two rubber tracks that stick well to the ice. Small wheels inside the tracks get power from two motors — one on each of the tracks.

Hanna and Heather built a remote control to run the robot from a safe place. The remote control tells the robot where to go and what to do. They put a special camera on it to look for victims trapped on the ice. The twins set up a TV to show where the robot goes to seek victims on the ice. A rope attached to the robot is used to tow victims back to safety.

The twins had to try out the robot many times because they had to make sure it would do the job. Hanna would pretend to be a victim, and Heather would **"rescue"** her sister over and over.

The Ice Crawler weighs only 23 pounds and is 4 feet long. "It works very well on hard ice or on soft snow," Heather exclaims. "It won't fall through."

---

rescue to save someone or something from danger or harm

The Ice Crawler won the twins a science prize and $50,000 to use for college.

Hanna and Heather toiled for two years. But when they were done, their zeal paid off. Ice Crawler won several top prizes! The twins are happy to gain fame, and it was a lot of fun to make the robot. But most of all, they hope their work will save lives in the cold parts of the world.

Word Find

Find these words. Circle them.
They may be down, slanted, or side-to-side.

Sounds like *dry* or *crazy*	Sounds like *dark*	Sounds like *cow* or *row*	Sounds like *later*
carry	smart	how	danger
happy	car	snow	water
very	hard	know	helper
only	part	tow	power
try		show	better

p	s	i	h	t	a	p	p	q	a	r	t
k	o	m	h	o	y	o	a	h	t	f	r
n	i	n	a	w	m	w	r	o	o	l	y
o	l	v	r	r	t	e	t	w	n	f	t
w	c	e	d	h	t	r	f	t	l	h	d
c	a	r	o	i	e	n	y	s	y	a	a
s	r	s	h	o	w	l	n	r	t	p	n
q	r	o	t	k	t	o	p	u	q	p	g
e	y	r	h	r	w	a	t	e	r	y	e
v	e	r	y	b	e	t	t	e	r	n	r

What Did You Read?

1. What idea did Hanna and Heather have?

   _____

   _____

2. Why is it important for helpers to get victims out of the cold water fast?

   _____

   _____

3. Why did the Ice Crawler have to be light?

   _____

   _____

4. What did Hanna and Heather use to tell the Ice Crawler where to go?

   _____

   _____

5. How did the twins know the Ice Crawler would work?

   _____

   _____